15 timeless classics

NEIL SEDAKA

Piano/vocal arrangements with guitar chord boxes

International Music Publications Ltd.

Arrangements and engraving by Artemis Music Limited
(www.artemismusic.com)
Photograph: Mick Hutson/Redferns Picture Library

Published 2005

CONTENTS

Breaking Up Is Hard To Do **18**
Calendar Girl **4**
Happy Birthday Sweet Sixteen **8**
I Go Ape **14**
(Is This The Way To) Amarillo **21**
King Of Clowns **26**
Laughter In The Rain **30**
Little Devil **33**
Little Lovin' **42**
Next Door To An Angel **38**
Oh Carol **47**
Our Last Song Together **50**
Stairway To Heaven **54**
Standing On The Inside **56**
That's When The Music Takes Me **61**

Calendar Girl

Words and Music by Howard Greenfield and Neil Sedaka

6

Happy Birthday Sweet Sixteen

Words and Music by Howard Greenfield and Neil Sedaka

you've turned in - to the pret - ti - est girl I've ev - er seen. ___

hap - py birth - day, sweet six - teen. ___

What hap - pened to ___ that fun - ny face? ___

My lit - tle tom - boy now wears sa - tins and lace, ___

I Go Ape

Words and Music by Howard Greenfield and Neil Sedaka

The moon is bright__ a-bove, oh what a night__ for__ love.

And as I hold__ you near, I whis-per in your ear.

I go ape ev-'ry time I see you smile,__ I'm a
I'm a mon-key's un-cle who's a cous-in to a chim-pan - zee,__ like I was
(Verse 3 see block lyric)

(Verse 3)
Honey you know that I'm gonna be true to you
I'll keep you in bananas and bring you coconuts too
And we'll settle down in the nearest county zoo.

Rama-langa...

Breaking Up Is Hard To Do

Words and Music by Howard Greenfield and Neil Sedaka

(Is This The Way To)Amarillo

Words and Music by Neil Sedaka and Howard Greenfield

King Of Clowns

Words and Music by Howard Greenfield and Neil Sedaka

Laughter In The Rain

Words and Music by Neil Sedaka and Philip Cody

Little Devil

Words and Music by Howard Greenfield and Neil Sedaka

34

They say be-ware but I don't care, I love you just the same.___ You're a

old heart - break - er and a mis - chief mak - er, but I'm wise to your game. Woah woah woah.

Hey lit - tle dev - il, I'm gon - na make an an - gel out - ta you.

Woah woah woah woah yeah yeah yeah, hey_____ you lit - tle dev - il.

Repeat to fade

(Verse 3)
Hey little devil everything is gonna be fine
'Cause someday soon I'm gonna make you all mine
There'll be no running around, you met your Waterloo
Hey little devil I'm gonna make an angel out of you.

Next Door To An Angel

Words and Music by Howard Greenfield and Neil Sedaka

Little Lovin'

Words and Music by Neil Sedaka and Philip Cody

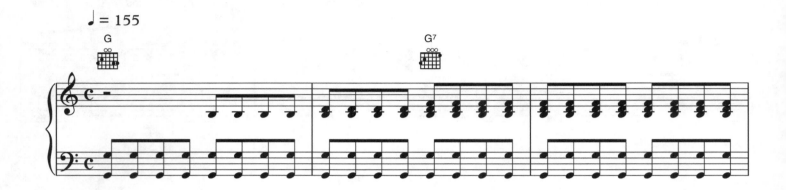

Ma - ma raised me to be a man,— told me 'son you have to
Un - cle Hen - ry and cou - sin Grace used to week - end—

(Verse 3 see block lyric)

un - der - stand.___ Learn to get while the get - tin's good,___
at our place.___ Grace and I would go a - round the barn,___

45

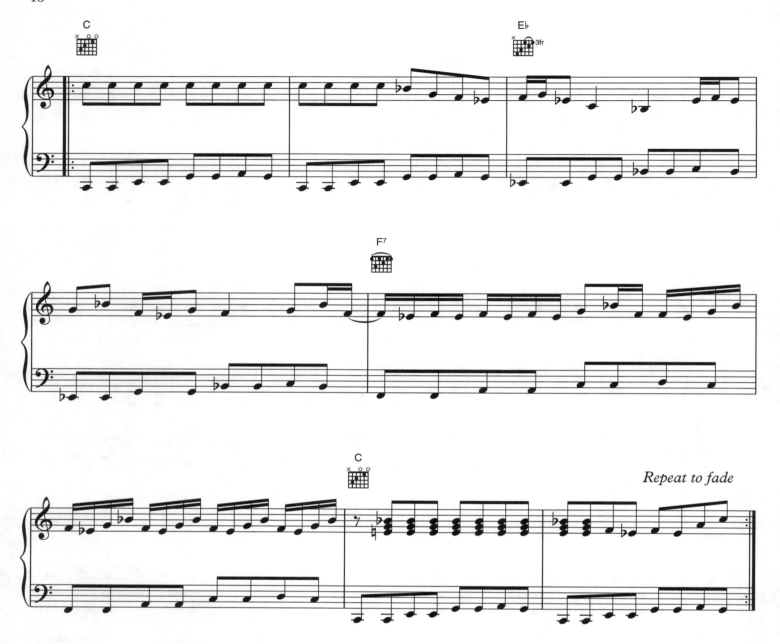

Repeat to fade

(Verse 3)
I knew a woman from New Orleans
Her old man used to treat her mean
And she would come to me for sympathy
Southern Comfort and ecstasy.

And I swear...

Oh Carol

Words and Music by Howard Greenfield and Neil Sedaka

2nd Verse: same lyrics as first, but spoken (rhythm ad.lib.)

Our Last Song Together

Words and Music by Howard Greenfield and Neil Sedaka

Stairway To Heaven

Words and Music by Howard Greenfield and Neil Sedaka

Climb up way up high._____ Climb up

way up high._____ Climb up way up high._____

Well-a-well a-well-a hea-ven-ly an-gel_____ I want you for my girl._____
Well-a-well-a-well-a o-ver the rain-bow, that's where I'm gon-na climb._____
Verse 3: Instrumental ad. lib.
Well-a-well-a-well-a got-ta be go-ing, gon-na leave world be-hind._____

Standing On The Inside

Words and Music by Neil Sedaka

Stan - ding on the out - side___ loo-kin' in.___

60

That's When The Music Takes Me

Words and Music by Neil Sedaka

That's when the mu - sic takes me, takes me to a brigh - ter day.

That's when the mu - sic takes me, hel - pin' me to find my way. And the day